I0200485

The Gospel According To
Orange Jesus

A Biblical Rationale for
Trump Derangement Syndrome*

As Reported by the "Fake" News

Illustrations by AI's a vast stream of ones and zeros
and a herd of Photoshop Guru's

And the cure for Trump Amnesia.

This is a work of parody. It is protected by U.S. copyright law as "fair use" (see 17 U.S. Code § 107). Any resemblance to actual persons, living or dead, or actual events is purely coincidental. The work is not intended to cause harm or infringe on the rights of the original creators. It is not officially endorsed or authorized by any parties associated with the originals.

The news articles may have been edited for length only. For full text, please refer to the original articles cited.

Headlines may have been substituted.

Illustrations by: Craiyon AI image generator

Copyright © 2024

All rights reserved. No part of this publication may be reproduced, distributed,or transmitted in any form or by any means, including photocopying, recording, or other electronic or mechanical methods, without the prior written permission of the publisher, except in the case of brief quotationsembodied in critical reviews and certain other non-commercial uses permitted by copyright law.

ISBN-13: 978-1-956688-25-2

The Gospel According to Orange Jesus

19 20 21 22 23 24 6 5 4 3 2 1

--

First Printing: 2024

Printed in the USA

Orange is the new Jumpsuit

Introduction:

A Biblical Rationale for Trump Derangement Syndrome

Donald "Orange Jesus" Trump was our first perfect President.
He singlehandedly has broken 10 out of 10 Commandments.
We've cited a series articles from the "Fake News" to document this.

Here is a handy checklist to help you follow along:

- ☐ 1. You shall have no other God's before me.
- ☐ 2. Thou shalt not make unto thee any graven images.
- ☐ 3. Thou shalt not take the name of the Lord thy God in vain.
- ☐ 4. Remember the Sabbath day and keep it Holy.
- ☐ 5. Honor your father and mother.
- ☐ 6. Thou shalt not kill.
- ☐ 7. Thou shalt not commit adultery.
- ☐ 8. Thou shalt not steal.
- ☐ 9. Thou shall not bear false witness.
- ☐ 10. You shall not covet.

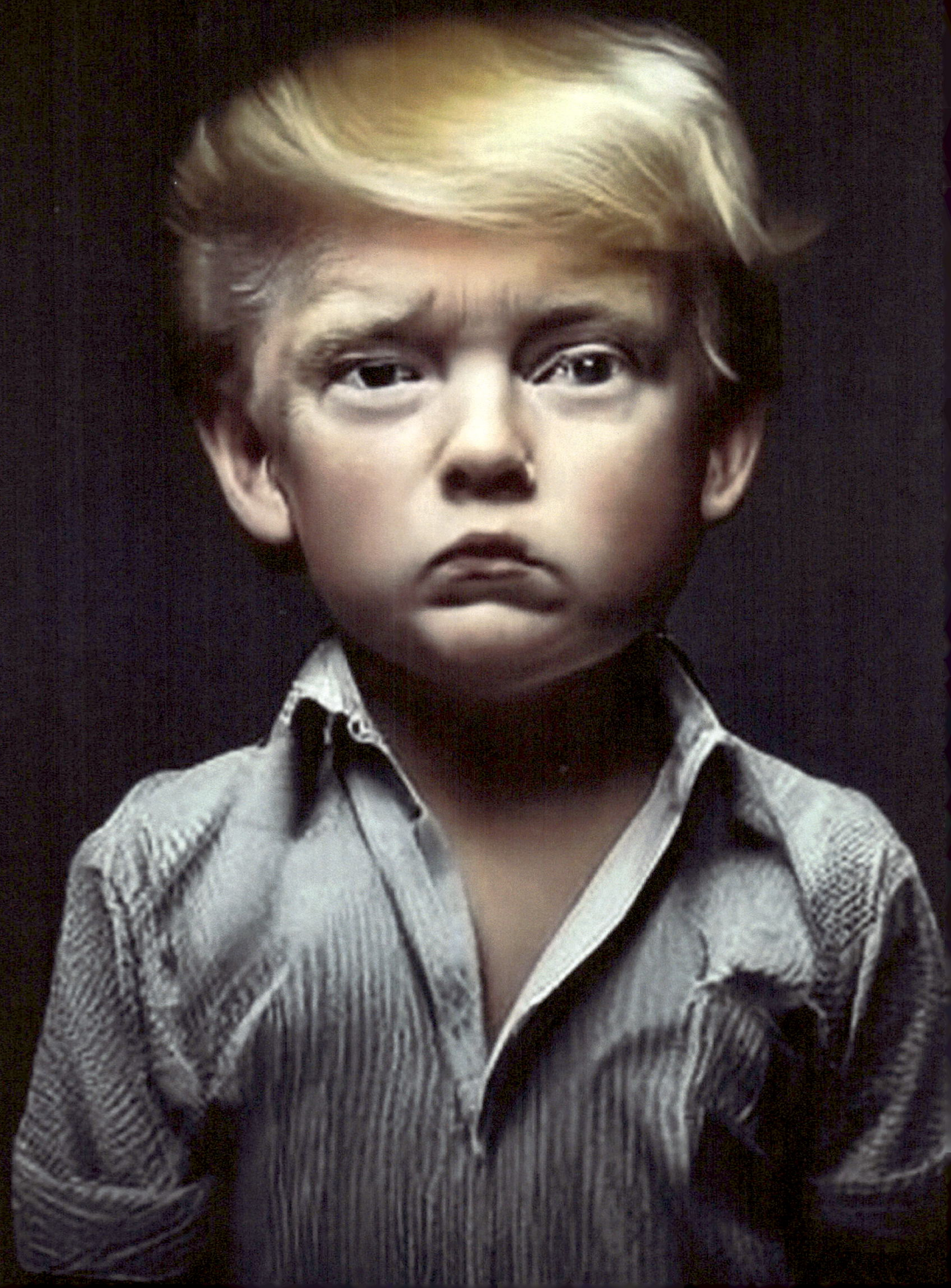

1st Commandment

I am the Lord thy God: Thou shalt not have strange Gods before me.

- Exodus 20:

Our new Messiah's birth announcement:

"And on 14 June 1946, God looked down on his planned paradise and said: 'I need a caretaker.'

"So God gave us Trump,"

"God said I need somebody willing to get up before dawn, fix this country, work all day, fight the Marxists, eat supper, then go to the Oval Office and stay past midnight at a meeting of the heads of state. So God made Trump,"

This is the narration from a video that comes from the Dilley Meme Team, a group of video creators that support Trump for president. It's called "God Made Trump" and it's played at some Trump campaign events.

"They've told me he's Jesus":

Unpacking Trump's empty pseudo-religion

By Chauncey DeVega, Salon, March 6, 2024

The most zealous and most extreme of MAGA supporters are white right-wing evangelical Christians, who have sought to identify Trump as a messiah or prophet, blessed and ordained by God as their weapon in an end-times battle against "evil," whose goal is to conquer American society, end multi-racial democracy, and transform the country into an authoritarian theocracy. These fantasies and delusions are shared, at least to some extent, by Trump himself.

Nothing can pull the radical white evangelicals away from Trump. They are hard-wired to see Trump as the only one who can set things right in America. The radical white evangelicals firmly believe (ordesperately hope) that there will be a moment of vindication that will prove their beliefs to be right. This will happen after Trump becomes leader for life in America, as some have openly stated. Trump perpetrates the same sense of retribution, equating his problems with theirs, cleverly including a reference to an epic apocalyptic battle with the "deep state" that is coming with the election. This rhetoric is dangerous, because it is not limited to online communications among believers but has spread to radical conservatives in the U.S. Congress.

Not everyone within MAGA circles believes Trump's outrageous statements about God and Jesus Christ but no one is offended. And of course, if we want to see historical precedents for this sacralization of the leader, the history of fascism tells us a lot about what Trump is doing. He is not original. Trump is simply following the fascist playbook of Hitler and Mussolini.

It's no accident that the theological rationales for supporting Trump have been all over the map. He's been cast as a modern-day messiah, as white evangelicals' own King Cyrus, or — my favorite—as a "baby Christian." This conceptual disarray is a clear indication that these are not rigorously developed religious rationales but rather theological fragments that are serving as backfill to support fealty to Trump. I think this is often missed. Most observers either take the theological language too seriously or dismiss it altogether.

But if you turn this kaleidoscope theology over enough, you can see that it is pointing to something bigger: the worldview of white Christian nationalism, the idea that the U.S. was designed by God to be a kind of promised land for European Christians.

The Orange Jesus Thing

We Stand at Armageddon...and we battle against the Lord?

Joe Klein, Sanity Clause Jan 11, 2024

Okay, this thing is getting pretty weird now. If you haven't seen the "God Made Trump" ad you absolutely must. I thought it was a joke at first —a parody ad you might see on Saturday Night Live. But it's not.

Trump's campaign is responsible for this satanic heresy. It represents a new level of craziness—the Orange Jesus thing made manifest. Trump is embracing his inner messiah. And it represents a certain reality in the Republican Party: I watched a clip of a Trump voter in Iowa the other day, a woman, who said—calmly, with the utter conviction of a mind-snatched cultist—that the legal cases against Big Orange were a sign from God that Trump had been sent to suffer for our sins.

We have entered the Elmer Gantry stage of the Trump candidacy. It's getting to be overtly religious.

And Trump himself seems to think he can walk on water. He can say any outrageous thing—that he hopes, for example, the economy will crash in the next year—without consequence.

This week he had his lawyers affirm in Washington's District Court of Appeals, that as President he could order Seal Team 6 to assassinate a political opponent and not be prosecuted for it unless he was tried and impeached by the Congress. And then there was the infamous Christmas message, a litany of people and things he hates—"lunatic" Jack Smith, electric cars etc and so forth—and the greeting: May they rot in hell.

Merry Christmas.

Do Americans have a 'collective amnesia' about Donald Trump?

By Jennifer Medina and Reid J. Epstein New York Times, March 5, 2024

Not all that long ago, many Americans committed hours a day to tracking then-President Donald Trump's every move. And then, sometime after the riot at the Capitol on Jan. 6, 2021, and before his first indictment, they largely stopped.

They are having trouble remembering it all again.

More than three years of distance from the daily onslaught has faded, changed – and in some cases, warped – Americans' memories of events that at the time felt searing. Polling suggests voters' views on Trump's policies and his presidency have improved in the rearview mirror. In interviews, voters often have a hazy recall of one of the most tumultuous periods in modern politics.

For now, the erosion of time appears to be working in Trump's favor, as swing voters base their support on their feelings about the present, not the past. "They know about what they don't like about Biden, and they have forgotten what they don't like about Trump."

Polls suggest that Mr. Trump has also made inroads with voters who may have been too young to remember his first term in detail. The nearly 4.2 million 18-year-olds who are newly eligible to vote this year were in middle school when Mr. Trump was first elected.

"Negative information about Trump is no longer distinctive, it is just the air that we breathe," Dr. Franks said. "It's the water that we are swimming in. It just becomes a conditioned emotional response, where you either feel joy and admiration or disgust and anger at the sight of his face — but each individual act is just a drop in the ocean."

"whoever exalts himself will be humbled"
~ Matthew 23:12

Cohen said Trump inflated his wealth as an ego booster, but it may have been a crime

By Kara Scannell, CNN, Thu February 28, 2019

Michael Cohen's depiction this week of how the Trump Organization manipulated figures to change the value of the company opened up the possibility that Donald Trump's strategy of using the illusion of vast wealth as an ego- and image-enhancing measure might also have been a crime.

In his public congressional testimony on Wednesday, Cohen indicated that his former client potentially committed a variety of financial crimes from bank to tax fraud in order to secure loans and even to move up in Forbes magazine's rankings of the very rich.

It's not clear whether Cohen's claims are being pursued by criminal investigators, but top Democratic Rep. Elijah Cummings, chair of the House Oversight Committee, said Wednesday that congressional committees are already divvying up the revelations for further investigation.

Cohen testified that, in 2014 when Trump was making a play for the Buffalo Bills football team, he provided financial statements to his long-time lender that his former attorney now claims were inflated.

Among the documents that Cohen provided to Congress were Trump's financial statements for the years 2011, 2012 and 2013. The documents showed a near doubling in Trump's net worth from $4.26 billion in 2011 and $4.56 billion 2012 to $8.66 billion in 2013. The leap was attributed to $4 billion in "brand value."

Donald John Trump, pictured on page 107
of his 1964 New York Military Academy yearbook

Captain Bone Spurs

Daughters of foot doctor say he diagnosed Trump with bone spurs as 'favor' to Fred Trump

by Veronica Stracqualursi, CNN, December 26, 2018

The daughters of a Queens foot doctor say their late father diagnosed President Donald Trump with bone spurs to help him avoid the Vietnam War draft as a "favor" to his father Fred Trump

Dr. Larry Braunstein, a podiatrist who died in 2007, often told the story of providing Donald Trump with the diagnosis of bone spurs in his heels so he could be exempt from military service, his two daughters – Dr. Elysa Braunstein and Sharon Kessel – told the New York Times.

Dr. Braunstein rented his office in Jamaica, Queens, from Fred Trump in the 1960s, the Times reported, citing records. His two daughters told the Times that their father provided the diagnosis of bone spurs as a courtesy to the elder Trump.

In 1968, after receiving four deferments due to education, Donald Trump was diagnosed with bone spurs in his heels at the age of 22, seven years before the Vietnam War ended.

• •

Sally Jackson, The Spokesman-Review, December 15, 2019

"Donald Trump chose not "to do what a man's go to do!" His dad got a doctor to say he had bone spurs on his feet, which kept him from serving his country. Well, "Captain Bone Spurs'" feet never kept him from walking hundreds of miles on multiple golf courses. Now "Captain Bone Spurs" is our draft-dodging commander in chief. That insults every man who had the guts to fight for our country."

Woe to those who plan iniquity

An Inflation Problem

Ruling Confirms Trump Used Fraud to Hype Property Values

by Heather Vogell, ProPublica, Sept. 29, 2023

New York State Supreme Court Justice Arthur Engoron, having previously made a preliminary finding that Trump, his sons and some Trump Organization executives "had a propensity to engage in persistent fraud by submitting false and misleading Statements of Financial Condition," granted a partial summary judgment in favor of the state of New York. "Even with a preliminary injunction in place," his lacerating opinion noted, "and with an independent monitor overseeing their compliance, defendants have continued to disseminate false and misleading information while conducting business."

The seeds of the state's case date back to 2019. In February of that year, former Trump lawyer Michael Cohen claimed in a congressional hearing that Trump had manipulated the values of his assets. "It was my experience that Mr. Trump inflated his total assets when it served his purposes, such as trying to be listed amongst the wealthiest people in Forbes," Cohen testified, "and deflated his assets to reduce his real estate taxes."

On Dec. 7, 2019, according to Engoron's ruling, New York Attorney General Letitia James subpoenaed the Trump Organization. Three years later, the state sued, claiming that Trump, his company and his associates grossly misstated the value of some of his properties on statements of financial condition shared with lenders and insurers. They included 40 Wall Street, Trump Tower, Trump Park Avenue, his Seven Springs Estate in Westchester, Mar-a-Lago and property near his Scottish golf course in Aberdeen.

In this week's ruling, Engoron called James' evidence "conclusive." Between 2014 and 2021, he wrote, Trump and others overvalued his assets by $812 million to $2.2 billion.

Are we little Gods?

Stormy Daniels' tell-all book on Trump: salacious detail and claims of cheating

Tom McCarthy, Guardian US, Tue 18 Sep 2018

The memoir narrates Daniels' first experiences as a stripper while still in high school, and how she broke into the porn industry, through which she rose to become an award-winning director, writer and star.

It was in that role that Daniels attended a celebrity golf tournament in Lake Tahoe, California, in 2006, where she and two colleagues greeted golfers between holes. There she first sees Trump: "He had a red cap, a Trump crest as a placeholder for the MAGA slogan not one of us could see coming."

Trump's bodyguard invites Daniels to dinner, which turns out to be an invitation to Trump's penthouse, she writes, in a description of alleged events that Daniels has disclosed previously but which in the book are rendered with new and lurid detail. She describes Trump's penis as "smaller than average" but 'not freakishly small."

"He knows he has an unusual penis," Daniels writes. "It has a huge mushroom head. Like a toadstool…

When you're the Messiah, they let you do it. You can do anything.

Grab 'em by the pussy. You can do anything."

Trump recorded having extremely lewd conversation about women in 2005

By David A. Fahrenthold, Washington Post, October 8, 2016

In this video from 2005, Donald Trump prepares for an appearance on 'Days of Our Lives' with Access Hollywood host Billy Bush and actress Arianne Zucker. (Video: Obtained by The Washington Post)

Donald Trump bragged in vulgar terms about kissing, groping and trying to have sex with women during a 2005 conversation caught on a hot microphone, saying that "when you're a star, they let you do it," according to a video obtained by The Washington Post.

The video captures Trump talking with Billy Bush, then of "Access Hollywood," on a bus with the show's name written across the side. They were arriving on the set of "Days of Our Lives" to tape a segment about Trump's cameo on the soap opera.

Late Friday night, following sharp criticism by Republican leaders, Trump issued a short video statement saying, "I said it, I was wrong, and I apologize." But he also called the revelation "a distraction from the issues we are facing today." He said that his "foolish" words are much different than the words and actions of Bill Clinton, whom he accused of abusing women, and Hillary Clinton, whom he accused of having "bullied, attacked, shamed and intimidated his victims."

"I could stand in the middle of 5th Avenue and shoot somebody."

(And my supporters will pay for it.)

By Katherine Doyle and Ben Kamisar, NBC News, Jan. 31, 2024

Former President Donald Trump's affiliated committees spent about $27 million on lawyers' bills and related legal fees in the last six months of 2023, new federal election filings show, bringing the total for a year that included four separate indictments to almost $50 million.

Trump's political fundraising apparatus is sprawling, but the new filings show that the price of lawyers is weighing him down. Still, Trump, the GOP presidential front-runner, has seized on the legal cases against him as a potent fundraising tool, with his booking in a Georgia election case giving him a record single-day haul.

Save America PAC, one of the groups Trump uses to raise money, spent $24.3 million on "legal consulting" in the last six months of 2023, a ccording to federal election filings. That includes payments to firms that include lawyers like John Lauro, who is representing Trump in the case related to his effort to overturn the 2020 election; Todd Blanche, who also represents Trump in the New York hush money case; and Alina Habba, who represents Trump in the defamation case filed against him by author E. Jean Carroll and has appeared at his criminal arraignments.

While the Save America PAC raised $36 million over the last six months, $30 million came across six monthly payments from Make America Great Again Inc., a Trump-affiliated super PAC. While Save America helped provide early funding for MAGA Inc. when it launched at the beginning of Trump's presidential bid, it appears that much of that money has been returned to Save America, which has been the primary vehicle for paying Trump's legal fees. In the first six months of 2023, Save America PAC took more than $12 million from MAGA Inc.

"when the doors were shut where the disciples were assembled, ... [Orange] Jesus came and stood in the midst"

John 20:19

Donald Trump 'just came strolling' into dressing rooms, pageant contestants allege

By Fred Barbash The Washington Post, October 12, 2016

On an April 11, 2005, Howard Stern show, Donald Trump bragged about some of the special perks he enjoyed while owner of the Miss USA pageant. They came not in a locker room but a dressing room.

"I'll go backstage before a show and everyone's getting dressed and ready and everything else," he said. "And you know, no men are anywhere. And I'm allowed to go in because I'm the owner of the pageant. And therefore I'm inspecting it."

Said Stern: "You're like a doctor."

Responded Trump: "Is everyone OK? You know they're standing there with no clothes. And you see these incredible looking women. And so I sort of get away with things like that."

CBS 2 Los Angeles did a little fact checking and, guess what, this time, no Pinocchios. Tasha Dixon, Miss Arizona of 2001, told the station that Trump just came "waltzing in" while contestants were nude or half-nude as they changed into bikinis.were naked.

Call Me Daddy

Donald Trump Fantasized About Having Sex With His Daughter Ivanka

Adrienne Mahsa Varkiani, The New Republic, June 28, 2023

Donald Trump regularly made lewd comments about his daughter Ivanka and fantasized about what it would be like to have sex with her, according to a former Trump administration official.

Trump's comments were part of a general culture of misogyny and sexism in the White House during his administration, Miles Taylor details in his upcoming book, Blowback: A Warning to Save Democracy From the Next Trump, which was first reported on by Newsweek on Wednesday.

"Aides said he talked about Ivanka Trump's breasts, her backside, and what it might be like to have sex with her, remarks that once led [former Chief of Staff] John Kelly to remind the president that Ivanka was his daughter," Taylor, who served as a Department of Homeland Security chief of staff under Trump, wrote in his book.

"Afterward, Kelly retold that story to me in visible disgust," Taylor writes. "Trump, he said, was 'a very, very evil man.'"

Taylor's allegations should not come as a huge shock, given the other disturbing things Trump has publicly said about his daughter.

In 2004, he told radio host Howard Stern that it was perfectly fine to refer to Ivanka as "a piece of ass."

In 2006, Trump engaged in another conversation with the radio host about the size of Ivanka's breasts. "She's actually always been very voluptuous," Trump said, telling Stern that she had not gotten breast implants. "She's tall, she's almost six feet tall and she's been, she's an amazing beauty."

DONALD
TRUMP

Trump Took $70,000 in Tax Deductions for Hair Care.

By James B. Stewart, The New York Times, Oct. 6, 2020

There were many bombshells in The New York Times's exposé last week about President Trump's taxes. He has paid basically zero federal income tax for years. His much-ballyhooed businesses are on the ropes. And that was just the headline.

But it was a juicy and seemingly less significant matter that jumped out at me: Mr. Trump spent more than $70,000 on hairstyling during several years of his run on "The Apprentice," his reality-TV show.

That, of course, is quite a lot for any one person to spend on having his hair cut, blow-dried or colored. But what is really remarkable about the revelation is that Mr. Trump's production company deducted his hairstyling expenses from its taxable income, reducing its tax bill.

Tax experts told me that deducting what is ordinarily considered a personal expense is prohibited under almost any circumstances. And they said such a deduction could potentially constitute criminal tax fraud if the cost of the hairstyling was reimbursed by someone else.

Three former NBC executives involved in "The Apprentice" told me that, while they didn't recall the exact terms of Mr. Trump's contract, they were very familiar with the way such contracts are typically written. The cost of hair and makeup for a star of Mr. Trump's stature would generally be covered by the show, and Mr. Trump would have been reimbursed for any of the costs he incurred.

"I can't think of any circumstances in which Trump would have paid those costs out of his own pocket and not be reimbursed," one of those officials said. The official spoke on the condition of anonymity because he still does business with NBC and Mark Burnett, the producer of "The Apprentice," who has also produced "The Voice" for NBC.

Taxpayers are not allowed to deduct reimbursed business expenses.

Two Corinthians, 3:17

"'The Art of the Deal' is second to the Bible."

Trump bungles Bible reference at Liberty University
Donald Trump bungles Bible reference at Liberty University

By Blake Hounshell - POLITICO 01/18/2016

Donald Trump, speaking to a religious crowd at Virginia's Liberty University on Monday, turned to Scripture.

"We're going to protect Christianity. I can say that. I don't have to be politically correct," he said. "Two Corinthians, 3:17, that's the whole ballgame … is that the one you like?"

The verse, "Now the Lord is that Spirit: and where the Spirit of the Lord is, there is liberty," seems to have been Trump's attempt to ingratiate himself to the audience of religious students.

But the crowd tittered, and several of the students audibly corrected him, pointing out that Christians say "Second Corinthians," not "Two Corinthians."

Trump later made his usual comparison between the Bible and "The Art of the Deal," his best-selling business book.

"'The Art of the Deal' is second to the Bible," Trump said magnanimously. As for other books, "The Bible blows them away. There's nothing like it, the Bible."

8th Commandment
Thou shall not bear false witnesss

The clear and present danger of Trump's enduring 'Big Lie'

By Melissa Block , NPR, December 23, 2021

Pro-Trump rioters storm the U.S. Capitol following a rally with President Donald Trump on Jan. 6. His supporters gathered in the nation's capital to protest the ratification of Joe Biden's Electoral College victory.

It's been nearly a year since the United States suffered an unprecedented attack on constitutional democracy. When a violent mob stormed the U.S. Capitol on Jan. 6, the goal was to overturn the results of the 2020 presidential election and install Donald Trump to a second term.

Call it an insurrection or a coup attempt, it was fueled by what's known as the "Big Lie": the verifiably false assertion that Trump won. Joe Biden won 306 votes in the Electoral College, while Trump received 232. In the popular vote, Biden won by more than 7 million votes.

Many are warning that over the past year, that "big lie" of a stolen election has grown more entrenched and more dangerous.

In rallies across the country, Trump continues to hammer on the fiction that the 2020 presidential election was stolen from him. Speaking at a rally in Georgia in September, Trump trumpeted his familiar, baseless claim that the election was "corrupt" and "rigged."

"I have no doubt that we won, and we won big," Trump said. "The headlines claiming that Biden won are fake news — and a very big lie." A couple of weeks later, he repeated the fiction at a rally in Iowa. "We didn't lose," he insisted to a crowd that rewarded him with chants of "Trump won!"

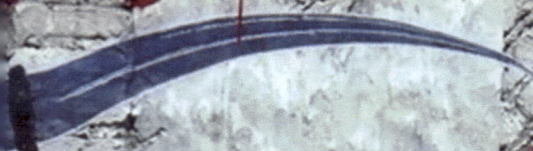

6th Commandment
Thou shalt not kill.

US could have averted 40% of Covid deaths, says panel examining Trump's policies

Amanda Holpuch, The Guardian, Feb 11, 2021

The country began the pandemic with a degraded public health infrastructure, leading to more deaths than other high-income countries

The US could have averted 40% of the deaths from Covid-19, had the country's death rates corresponded with the rates in other high-income G7 countries, according to a Lancet commission tasked with assessing Donald Trump's health policy record.

Almost 470,000 Americans have died from the coronavirus so far, with the number widely expected to go above half a million in the next few weeks. At the same time some 27 million people in the US have been infected. Both figures are by far the highest in the world.

In seeking to respond to the pandemic, Trump has been widely condemned for not taking the pandemic seriously enough soon enough, spreading conspiracy theories, not encouraging mask wearing and undermining scientists and others seeking to combat the virus's spread.

In a wide-ranging assessment published on Thursday, the commission said Trump "brought misfortune to the USA and the planet" during his four years in office. The stinging critique not only blamed Trump, but also tied his actions to the historical conditions which made his presidency possible.

In another comparison, the commission found if US life expectancy was equivalent to the average in the other G7 countries, 461,000 fewer Americans would have died in 2018.

Cross-Dresser

A jury in a civil case has found former President Donald Trump sexually abused a magazine columnist in a New York department store in the 1990s. But Mr Trump was found not liable for raping E Jean Carroll in the dressing room of Bergdorf Goodman.

Everyone keeps asking the wrong question.
They keep asking did you rape E. Jean Carroll?

Of course he did because when you're a celebrity, you can do anything.

Perhaps the real question should be, why were you in the Bergdorf Goodman ladies dressing room in the first place?

6th Commandment

"Thou shalt not commit adultery."

✝ Exodus 20:14

Kate Taylor and Erin Snodgrass, Business Insider, Apr 4, 2023

Melania gave birth to the couple's only son, Barron, in March 2006. Adult film star Stormy Daniels alleged that she and Trump had a sexual encounter just four months later, in July 2006.

In January 2018, the Wall Street Journal reported that Trump's personal lawyer, Michael Cohen, had facilitated a $130,000 payment to Daniels, whose real name is Stephanie Clifford, shortly before the 2016 election.

In August 2018, Cohen pleaded guilty to eight federal crimes, including making an illegal campaign contribution on the same day he facilitated the payment to Daniels.

Fast-forward five years, and a New York grand jury has voted to indict Trump, capping the Manhattan district attorney's office yearslong investigation into Trump's personal and business finances. The charges are likely linked to the $130,000 payment to Daniels.

Photo: Wikipedia

I'm not a puppet,
but Putin has his hand all the way up my butt.

The internet can't get over Donald Trump's response to being called a "puppet"

By Jennifer Earl, CBS News, October 19, 2016

It's clear Donald Trump did not enjoy being called a "puppet" during the final presidential debate on Wednesday by Hillary Clinton as she discussed his relationship with Russian President Vladimir Putin.

"Everything I see, [Putin] has no respect for this person," Trump said.

"Well, that's because he'd rather have a puppet as president of the United States," Clinton fired back.

"No puppet. No Puppet," said Trump, shaking his head.

"It's pretty clear...," Clinton continued, as Trump interrupted: "You're the puppet!"

Trump later said that he's never even met Putin, and that he "is not my best friend."

But by that point, Twitter users were already sharing photos and memes of puppets to mimic his response, using the phrase: "NO YOU'RE THE PUPPET."

There were already more than 35,000 tweets about the topic by the end of the first half of the debate. It was also the "top moment" of the debate by 9:45 p.m. ET, according to Facebook.

And the internet is loving it.

"'NO, YOU'RE THE PUPPET!' A presidential candidate just went straight up preschool on his opponent," one person tweeted.

Pointing to his head, Mr Trump went on: "I'm not a doctor.
But I'm, like, a person that has a good you-know-what."

Therefore, since we have these promises, dear friends, let us purify ourselves from everything that contaminates body and spirit, perfecting holiness out of reverence for God.

✝ 2 Corinthians 7:1

President Donald Trump suggested the possibility of an "injection" of disinfectant into a person infected with the coronavirus as a deterrent to the virus during his daily briefing.

By Dartunorro Clark, NBC News, April 23, 2020

Trump made the remark after Bill Bryan, who leads the Department of Homeland Security's science and technology division, gave a presentation on research his team has conducted that shows that the virus doesn't live as long in warmer and more humid temperatures. Bryan said, "The virus dies quickest in sunlight," leaving Trump to wonder whether you could bring the light "inside the body."

"So supposing we hit the body with a tremendous — whether it's ultraviolet or just a very powerful light — and I think you said that hasn't been checked because of the testing," Trump said, speaking to Bryan during the briefing. "And then I said, supposing you brought the light inside the body, which you can do either through the skin or some other way, and I think you said you're going to test that, too."

He added: "I see the disinfectant that knocks it out in a minute, one minute. And is there a way we can do something like that by injection inside or almost a cleaning? As you see, it gets in the lungs, it does a tremendous number on the lungs, so it would be interesting to check that."

He didn't specify the kind of disinfectant.

Medical professionals, including Dr. Vin Gupta, a pulmonologist, global health policy expert and an NBC News and MSNBC contributor. were quick to challenge the president's "improper health messaging."

"This notion of injecting or ingesting any type of cleansing product into the body is irresponsible and it's dangerous," said Gupta. "It's a common method that people utilize when they want to kill themselves."

He can turn water into carbonated sugar water with the push of a button

Trump Hired Diet Coke Valet Despite Sexual Misconduct

By Margaret Hartmann, Intelligencer Feb. 2, 2024

When we first learned of Donald Trump's Diet Coke valet about 100 days into his presidency, he was just a guy who would come running with fizzy aspartame water whenever the "leader of the free world" pressed a red button on the Resolute Desk — an event that might occur a dozen times a day.

After Trump left office, we discovered that the valet's name is Walt Nauta, and that he'd become one of the former president's closest aides; eventually, he would also become his co-defendant in the classified-documents case. After serving Trump as a military valet in the White House, Nauta joined him at Mar-a-Lago as his "personal aide and general gofer." A March 2023 Washington Post profile depicted the Navy veteran as subservient, extremely loyal to Trump, and uniquely uninterested in stabbing colleagues in the back to advance himself. "Some staffers who worked in the White House with Nauta recalled that in the freewheeling world of the Trump administration, he was one of the few staffers who appeared to perform his role — no more, no less," the paper reported.

But maybe, despite his apparent competence, Nauta is less of a rarity than he initially seemed. The Daily Beast reported on Friday that Nauta — like his boss and many other Trump-world figures — has been accused of sexual harassment by multiple women. The allegations against Nauta, which three female servicemembers reported to their supervisors in spring 2021, led to him being swiftly reassigned.

Three-ring circus

"The man who hates and divorces his wife," says the Lord, the God of Israel, "does violence to the one he should protect."

– Malachi 2:16

Donald Trump has been married to Melania Trump since 2005, but he was married twice before. His first marriage to model Ivana Trump in 1977 gave him three of his five kids — Donald Jr., Ivanka, and Eric — and the couple was very much a part of New York's social scene throughout the 1980s.

But their marriage devolved into a very public and very messy split with Donald and Ivana's divorce finalized in 1992. In the divorce, Ivana got $14 million and two luxury properties, including a Trump Plaza apartment, and $650,000 a year for their three kids.

A large part of the reason for the marriage breaking down was the arrival of the woman who would become Donald's second wife — Marla Maples. Marla and Donald had an affair in the early 1990s while he was married to Ivana, and they got married in 1993 a couple of months after the birth of their daughter Tiffany Trump.

But less than four years after tying the knot, Donald and Marla were separated, and their divorce was official by 1999. With their prenuptial agreement, Marla got much less than Ivana — $1 million in cash and $1 million to buy a house with $100,000 a year for child support until Tiffany turned 21. In 1998, as the divorce between Marla and Donald was being finalized, Donald started dating model Melania Knauss, who would become his third wife. They now have a son, Barron Trump.

He performs miracles by the laying on of his tiny hands

The History Behind the Donald Trump 'Small Hands' Insult

By ABC News, March 4, 2016

Marco Rubio told supporters last week that GOP presidential rival Donald Trump is "always calling me 'little Marco.' He is taller than me, he's like 6' 2", which is why I don't understand why his hands are the size of someone who is 5' 2"," Rubio joked. "Have you seen his hands? And you know what they say about men with small hands -- You can't trust them," Rubio said.

Nearly 30 years ago, Graydon Carter, the editor of Vanity Fair magazine, described Trump in Spy magazine as a "short-fingered vulgarian."

In an editor's letter in "Vanity Fair" last November, Carter said that he wrote the Sky magazine comment in 1988 "just to drive him a little bit crazy." And according to Carter, it still does.

"Like so many bullies, Trump has skin of gossamer," Carter wrote in November. "To this day, I receive the occasional envelope from Trump. There is always a photo of him—generally a tear sheet from a magazine. On all of them he has circled his hand in gold Sharpie in a valiant effort to highlight the length of his fingers," Carter wrote. "I almost feel sorry for the poor fellow because, to me, the fingers still look abnormally stubby."

Trump has brought up his hands up at least twice in the past 24 hours.

"Look at those hands," Trump said on the debate stage, holding up his hands to the audience. "Are they small hands? And he referred to my hands -- if they are small, something else must be small."

"I guarantee you there is no problem," Trump affirmed. "I guarantee you."

Sticks and Stones

Vulgarities, insults, baseless attacks: Trump backers follow his lead

By Hannah Knowles, Waashington Post, November 19, 2023

Many GOP voters are not just tolerating, but relishing and emulating Trump's often crass and cruel approach to politics.

Trump's coarseness and cruelty have come to define the Republican Party since his rise to the presidency — and many GOP voters relish and emulate the approach, while others tolerate it. The split-screen on display in Iowa on Friday and Saturday highlighted one of the defining dynamics in the Republican race, in which Trump is the dominant polling leader overshadowing a roster of candidates running more traditional campaigns.

Trump's rhetoric has alienated voters across the political spectrum and made him a particularly galvanizing opponent for Democrats. Within the GOP, however, it has spread, with others down the ballot and even some of his rivals looking to replicate his shock tactics. Saturday afternoon's event in Fort Dodge served as a stark illustration of the crudeness, meanness and unfounded accusations that he has helped normalize in politics.

The substance and tone of Trump's event was typical for a candidate who shot to political power with shocking pronouncements, insulting tweets and breaches of basic etiquette that, to supporters, were proof of his pitch as an outsider rather than a standard politician. He gained a political following pushing false claims that the country's first Black president was born in Africa, denigrated migrants from certain countries, gave cutting nicknames to his rivals and enemies and won despite a recording in which he bragged in crass terms about groping women.

"Everything Donald Trump says is either projection or a reflection of his deep insecurities. The American people elected Joe Biden in 2020 and rejected the hateful, divisive extremism of Trump and the MAGA Republicans, and they'll do it again next November," said Biden campaign spokesman Ammar Moussa.

Love,
Kim

XOXOXO

"And then we fell in love"

Trump's Bromance with Kim Is Gross, But Let the Love Letters Continue

By John Feffer, Foriegn Policy in Focus, March 5, 2019

Of all the bizarre things that Donald Trump utters — the lies, the garbled words, the fanciful stories — his comments on his relationship with North Korean leader Kim Jong Un are in a category by themselves.

"I was really tough and so was he, and we went back and forth," Trump told a crowd of supporters in West Virginia in September. "And then we fell in love, OK? No, really, he wrote me beautiful letters, and they're great letters. We fell in love."

Trump has bragged about these letters, has shown them to foreign visitors. The two leaders seem to enjoy a mutual personality cult that goes beyond even the friendships that Trump has cultivated with other authoritarian leaders like Russia's Vladimir Putin and Saudi Arabia's Mohammed bin Salman.

So, expectations were high that Trump and Kim would consummate their relationship at a second summit in Vietnam and produce something of lasting importance: denuclearization, removal of economic sanctions, a peace declaration, an exchange of liaison offices.

But the two leaders didn't even stay for the full meeting. They passed up a final lunch together and skipped the statement signing. The food left uneaten was statement enough. What was supposed to be the crowning achievement of Trump's foreign policy, the one-and-only rationale for his receiving a Nobel Peace Prize, has turned into a high-profile embarrassment.

ne Doria orecast Trac

Note: The cone contains the probable path of the storm center the size of the storm. Hazardous conditions can occur outsid

NC

SC

AL

GA

FL

8 AM Tue

8 AM Sun

8 AM Sat

8 PM Fri

8 AM

H

M

M

M

M

M

M

8 AM Mon

H

Bahamas

Cuba

Halti

Dominican Republic

Puerto

Jamaica

85W   80W   75W   70W

Dorian
ust 29, 2019
dvisory 21
Hurricane

Current information: ✗
Center location 21.4 N 67.2 W
Maximum sustained wind 85 mph

Forec
● Trop
Sustain

He can control the weather with a flick of a Sharpie.

Many heads got scratched this week when President Trump doubled down on his erroneous claim that Alabama had been in the path of Hurricane Dorian.

Apparently relying on a map that warned of high winds, or another showing hypothetical paths for the storm, the president over the weekend insisted Alabama was "in the crosshairs." At midweek, sitting in the Oval Office, he held up a map on which someone using a marking pen had ballooned the area of actual hurricane threat to include Alabama.

The question had to be asked: wouldn't it be enough to be worried about Florida, Georgia and the rest of the southeastern coast without dragging in Alabama – a state outside the current danger zone?

Perhaps. But in seeking to understand the moment it was tempting to observe that Alabama is arguably the cornerstone of the president's base of support in seeking a second term.

Simply Brilliant

When science gets in his way, Trump is happy to attack or distort it—or block it altogether. His administration kicked scientists off EPA advisory panels, replacing them with allies who questioned the need to regulate smog and greenhouse gases. It canceled a $1 million study on the risks of mountaintop-removal coal mining. It stopped funding children's health centers that studied the impact of pollution.

The pandemic, of course, is where Trump's willful and wishful ignorance turned the most deadly. Even as he privately acknowledged the danger of the novel coronavirus in February 2020, he publicly proclaimed that it would "go away" as the weather warmed. When that didn't happen, Trump tried new ways to downplay the virus's threat. He promoted miracle cures: first hydroxychloroquine and then convalescent plasma, diverting federal resources to drugs that did nothing against the virus. He mocked masks. When the vaccines finally arrived, he endorsed only half-heartedly what should have been his administration's crowning scientific achievement, because admitting that the shots were a big deal would have meant admitting that the virus was a big deal.

•••

The President Who Looked at the Sun

By James Hamblin, The Atlantic, August 21, 2017

During the solar eclipse today, President Donald Trump stepped onto the White House balcony with his wife and his son Barron, and he looked up at the sun.

According to White House reporters, an aide shouted a warning that he should not look at the sun. Nevertheless, he persisted. There were parts of the United States, along path of totality, that allowed people to look directly at the eclipse. But Washington, D.C., was not among them.

The Church of Orange Jesus has a choir

The 26 women who have accused Trump of sexual misconduct

By Eliza Relman and Azmi Haroun, Business Insider, May 9, 2023

A deluge of women made their accusations public following the October 2016 publication of the "Access Hollywood" tape, in which Trump was heard boasting about grabbing women's genitals in 2005. Some of Trump's accusers made their stories public months before the tape's release, and still others came forward in the months following.

Trump has broadly dismissed the allegations, which include harassment, groping, and rape, as "fabricated" and politically motivated accounts pushed by the media and his political opponents. In 2016, he promised to sue all of his accusers. In some cases, Trump and his lawyers have suggested he couldn't have engaged in the alleged behavior with certain women because he wasn't physically attracted to them.

"Every woman lied when they came forward to hurt my campaign," the Republican presidential nominee said during a 2016 rally. "Total fabrication. The events never happened. Never. All of these liars will be sued after the election is over."

The president said these "false allegations" against him were made by "women who got paid a lot of money to make up stories about me." And then alleged that the "mainstream media" refused to report evidence that the accusations were made up.

Trump has not yet made good on his promise to sue any of the women — although two women have sued him — and the White House says that Trump's election proves the American people don't consider the allegations disqualifying.

fat Elvis

Trump asked his followers if they think he looks like Elvis in a strange social media post

Alia Shoaib – Business Insider, Feb 4, 2024

Trump asked his followers on Truth Social whether he resembles the King of Rock and Roll. He shared a photo of half of his face spliced with Elvis Presley's. The post was widely mocked on social media and sparked questions about his state of mind.

Former President Donald Trump shared a strange post on social media asking his followers if they think he resembles Elvis Presley. In a post on Truth Social on Saturday, Trump shared a photo of half of his face spliced with the King of Rock and Roll's face. He wrote: "For so many years, people have been saying that Elvis and I look alike. Now this pic has been going all over the place. What do you think?"

Many took to social media to mock Trump for the random comparison.

An X account called Republicans against Trump simply posted a definition of narcissistic personality disorder in response.

Democratic strategist Johnny Palmadessa also took to X to question Trump's state of mind.

"Donald Trump clearly has dementia," he wrote.

Palmadessa listed a series of blunders Trump has made on the campaign trail, including speaking about former President Barack Obama as if he is still in office and mixing up his GOP rival Nikki Haley with former House Speaker Nancy Pelosi.

Some responders on Trump's platform, Truth Social, validated his suspicion that he does resemble Elvis — although some mocked him by editing photos to compare his face to Adolf Hitler and an oompa loompa.

A tale as old as time

Donald Trump, a Playboy Model, and a System for Concealing Infidelity

By Ronan Farrow, The New Yorker, February 16, 2018

In June, 2006, Donald Trump taped an episode of his reality-television show, "The Apprentice," at the Playboy Mansion, in Los Angeles. Hugh Hefner, Playboy's publisher, threw a pool party for the show's contestants with dozens of current and former Playmates, including Karen McDougal, a slim brunette who had been named Playmate of the Year, eight years earlier. In 2001, the magazine's readers voted her runner-up for "Playmate of the '90s," behind Pamela Anderson. At the time of the party, Trump had been married to the Slovenian model Melania Knauss for less than two years; their son, Barron, was a few months old. Trump seemed uninhibited by his new family obligations. McDougal later wrote that Trump "immediately took a liking to me, kept talking to me - telling me how beautiful I was, etc. It was so obvious that a Playmate Promotions exec said, 'Wow, he was all over you - I think you could be his next wife.'"

Trump and McDougal began an affair... McDougal describes their affair as entirely consensual. But her account provides a detailed look at how Trump and his allies used clandestine hotel-room meetings, payoffs, and complex legal agreements to keep affairs—sometimes multiple affairs he carried out simultaneously—out of the press.

On November 4, 2016, four days before the election, the Wall Street Journal reported that American Media, Inc., the publisher of the National Enquirer, had paid a hundred and fifty thousand dollars for exclusive rights to McDougal's story, which it never ran. Purchasing a story in order to bury it is a practice that many in the tabloid industry call "catch and kill." This is a favorite tactic of the C.E.O. and chairman of A.M.I., David Pecker, who describes the President as "a personal friend."

Our Bodies Belong To God, We Should Honor Him with It.

1 Corinthians 6:19⋅20 –

By Adam Gabbatt, Sat 3 Oct 2020

On Friday morning, ex-White House doctor Ronny Jackson confidently told Fox News that Donald Trump was not exhibiting any symptoms from coronavirus. Donald J Trump spars with his Democratic presidential rival Joe Biden in Cleveland, Ohio on Tuesday.

Shortly after, a White House official came forward to confirm that Trump was, actually, experiencing symptoms – albeit minor ones – and reports said Trump had appeared tired on Wednesday and "seemed lethargic" on Thursday. On Friday afternoon he was taken to Walter Reed military hospital.

"If elected, Mr Trump, I can state unequivocally, will be the healthiest individual ever elected to the presidency," Harold Bornstein wrote in December 2015.

The letter gushed that Trump's "physical strength and stamina are extraordinary", and his bloodwork was "astonishingly excellent".

Nearly three years later Bornstein confessed that Trump had dictated the note himself, but the skulduggery over Trump's wellbeing did not end there.

Bornstein also claimed that Trump's longtime bodyguard, Keith Schiller, had conducted a "raid" on his office in February 2017, scooping up Trump's medical charts and lab reports.

The gushing dispatch about Trump's fitness wasn't the last doctor's note to be questioned.In 2018 Jackson reported that Donald Trump weighed in at 239lb during his annual medical exam. That put Trump a pound shy of being obese. But in Jackson's report, he had clocked Trump as being 6ft 3in tall – meaning the president had apparently grown an inch since 2012, when his driving license listed him as 6ft 2in.

May the mountains sing together for joy

Psalm 98:8

Yes, of course Donald Trump wants his face added to Mount Rushmore

by Chris Cillizza, CNN Editor-at-large, Mon August 10, 2020

On Sunday night, President Donald Trump tweeted out a picture of himself standing in front of Mount Rushmore – an image that made him look as though he was the fifth presidential bust on the iconic monument.

Moments later, he tweeted out a sort-of denial of a New York Times report that he had spoken with South Dakota Gov. Kristi Noem about the possibility of adding his own visage to those of George Washington, Thomas Jefferson, Theodore Roosevelt and Abraham Lincoln.

We know that Trump has, in fact, raised the topic with Noem and that he was serious about it.

"He said, 'Kristi, come on over here. Shake my hand,'" Noem told the Sioux Falls Argus-Leader about a meeting with Trump in the Oval Office. "I shook his hand, and I said, 'Mr. President, you should come to South Dakota sometime. We have Mount Rushmore.' And he goes, 'Do you know it's my dream to have my face on Mount Rushmore?'. "I started laughing. He wasn't laughing, so he was totally serious."

He's not joking. Remember that Trump always uses the I-am-just-joking-and-you-media-stiffs-don't-get-it explanation whenever he says something that a) he means and b) he wants to give himself the ability to walk away from. But he's not joking. Not at all.

"In private, the efforts to charm Mr. Trump were more pointed, according to a person familiar with the episode: Ms. Noem greeted him with a four-foot replica of Mount Rushmore that included a fifth presidential likeness: his."

She had a Mount Rushmore replica made with Trump's face on it!

3rd Commandment

"Remember the sabbath day, to keep it holy."

By MJ Lee, CNN Politics, June 2017

Trump is unique among modern American presidents for his seeming lack of deep religious orientation. He doesn't have a hometown church, and a months-long examination of the congregations he had ties to throughout his life found no evidence that Trump put down permanent roots in any of them. Congregants at his childhood church in Queens say Trump might not be welcome there today. The midtown Manhattan church he attended later in life has denied that he is a member there, and the son of its famous pastor, Norman Vincent Peale, has denounced Trump.

Soon after announcing his presidential bid, Trump described the experience of taking Communion as, "When I drink my little wine -- which is about the only wine I drink -- and have my little cracker." In that same interview, Trump remarked that he wasn't sure he had ever asked God for forgiveness.

At another point in Trump's life, he might have looked to a different church in midtown Manhattan. After attending First Presbyterian in Queens, Trump and his family eventually switched to Marble Collegiate, home to Peale, a famous pastor.

When Trump told reporters that he attended Marble, the church took the rare step of publicly rejecting that claim, saying in a statement that Trump was "not an active member" of the church.

Thou shall not have bad hair days.

Trump: Americans Who Died in War Are 'Losers' and 'Suckers'

By Jeffrey Goldberg, The Atlantic, September 3, 2020

When President Donald Trump canceled a visit to the Aisne-Marne American Cemetery near Paris in 2018, he blamed rain for the last-minute decision, saying that "the helicopter couldn't fly" and that the Secret Service wouldn't drive him there. Neither claim was true.

Trump rejected the idea of the visit because he feared his hair would become disheveled in the rain, and because he did not believe it important to honor American war dead, according to four people with firsthand knowledge of the discussion that day. In a conversation with senior staff members on the morning of the scheduled visit, Trump said, "Why should I go to that cemetery? It's filled with losers." In a separate conversation on the same trip, Trump referred to the more than 1,800 marines who lost their lives at Belleau Wood as "suckers" for getting killed.

Belleau Wood is a consequential battle in American history, and the ground on which it was fought is venerated by the Marine Corps. America and its allies stopped the German advance toward Paris there in the spring of 1918. But Trump, on that same trip, asked aides, "Who were the good guys in this war?" He also said that he didn't understand why the United States would intervene on the side of the Allies.

Up against the wall that Mexico is paying for.

Border Walls are Symbols of Failure

By: Eric Schewe, JSTOR Daily, February 28, 2019

The American political system is now seized by conflict over the symbolic threat of illegal immigration. President Trump has proposed an equally symbolic solution—building a bigger border wall. Interestingly, while vilifying illegal immigrants to his supporters as violent criminals, he has not penalized the industries that rely on their labor. After settling the budget standoff that shuttered the federal government for a month, he declared a national emergency to fund wall construction, although he immediately admitted there was no emergency—that he "didn't need to do this."

Congress passed the 2006 Secure Fence Act with support from Senators Clinton, Biden, and Obama that expanded the border fence to 650 miles.

Despite Democrats' current reluctance to provide any further funding for the wall, the U.S.-Mexico border fence as it stands today began as a bipartisan project. In a post-9/11 surge of security concern, Congress passed the 2006 Secure Fence Act with support from Senators Clinton, Biden, and Obama that expanded the border fence from covering about a hundred miles around urban areas to 650 miles.

Erecting physical barriers is much easier than addressing the economic and political causes of migration under duress. Barriers do not work. In fact, they are a symbol that the system has already failed.

The wall was one of the premier technologies of the feudal era. In an age of fractured sovereignty, with aristocratic privilege confronting mass poverty, a fortress was a fitting defense for the main tool of politics—violent force. This was an era of smaller polities, towns, and cities that could be completely surrounded by walls. Prior to the invention of gunpowder, these walls could actually keep out invading forces, and with adequate resources, withstand sieges.

Yet according to archaeology scholar Ross Samson, walls were just as useful symbolically, in an era that placed huge importance on physical signs.

Witch Hunt

Trump claims the New York, Georgia, Florida, and District of Columbia criminal cases—with 91 felony charges—are politically motivated to restrict his ability to run for president in 2024.

Anyone would realize the hypocrisy of Trump's ploy if they knew he never declared "witch hunt" in the 62 lawsuits he filed and lost while contesting the 2020 election. Note: Trump-appointed judges were among the 80-plus magistrates who dismissed his election fraud lawsuits.

Crowd:
A witch! A witch! A witch!
We found a witch! We've got a witch! A witch! A witch!
We have found a witch. May we burn her?
- How do you know she is a witch
- She looks like one.
- Bring her forward.
- I'm not a witch! I'm not a witch !
- But you are dressed as one.
- They dressed me like this. - No, we didn't.
- And this isn't my nose. It's a false one.
- Well? - We did do the nose.
- The nose? - And the hat. But she is a witch !
- Did you dress her up like this? - No, no!
- Yes. A bit.
- She has got a wart.
- What makes you think she's a witch?
- She turned me into a newt!
- A newt?
- I got better.
- Burn her anyway!

– from Monty Python and the Holy Grail (1975)

"Oh, look at my African American over here"

- Donald Trump, September 13, 2020

Trump sneakers an effort to connect with Black voters

Elizabeth Beyer, USA TODAY, February 24, 2024

Fox News contributor Raymond Arroyo doubled down on a racial trope that Black Americans will support former President Donald Trump because "they love sneakers."

Last week, the GOP frontrunner made a surprise visit to Sneaker Con in Philadelphia to debut red, blue, and gold gym shoes called "Never Surrender High Top Sneaker," selling for $399.

"This is (the shoes) connecting with Black America. Because they're into sneakers. They love sneakers. This is a big deal. Certainly in the inner city," Fox News contributor Raymond Arroyo said during a network broadcast.

Arroyo suggested that Black voters will pivot from the Democratic Party and President Joe Biden because of the new footwear.

"It's for people who want Donald Trump-brand sneakers that, against, he's connecting on a different level."

More:Hey Fox News: The gold Trump sneakers are ugly. And they won't sway the Black vote.

The nearly $400 sneakers were released the day after a judge ordered Trump and his namesake company to pay $453.5 million in a New York real estate fraud lawsuit.

White Supremacists And Me,
𝔄 𝔏𝔬𝔳𝔢 𝔖𝔱𝔬𝔯𝔶

"These people love me. These are my people."

By Bess Levin, Vanity Fair, September 16, 2021

Say what you will about Donald Trump, but the man has always said that everyone should be treated equally, no matter the religion they practice or the color of their skin, and in his four years in the White House, he never once gave anyone any reason to believe he had a single ounce of prejudice in his body.

Just kidding, of course. The man is and always has been an out and out racist, and while the examples to back this up are too numerous to mention, just a small sampling includes calling for the execution of five Black and Latino teenagers; telling four congresswoman of color to "go back" to the "totally broken and crime infested places from which they came," when three-quarters of the group "came from" the U.S.; helping start an entire movement around the lie that the country's first Black president wasn't born here; and describing Baltimore, whose population is majority Black, as a "disgusting, rat and rodent infested mess" where "no human being" would "want to live."

But wait, you say, what about the time he banned travel to the U.S. from seven predominantly Muslim nations? Or called Mexicans rapists and criminals? Or pardoned a guy a U.S. Department of Justice expert said oversaw the worst pattern of racial profiling by a law enforcement agency in U.S. history? Or threw an absolute shit fit over the removal of statue of a Confederate general who thought Black people should be white people's property, insisting said general was one of the greatest military leaders of all time? Obviously, if we were to include everything, we'd be here all day.

"most manly, most masculine, most handsome mug shot of all time."

–ex-Trump spokesman Hogan Gidley

The New York Times fashion critic Vanessa Friedman called the image "a mug shot for history that is unprecedented" and noted that "his face is lit from above by a blinding white flash that hits his ash blond hair like a spotlight. [...] He glowers out from beneath his brows, unsmiling, eyes rendered oddly bloodshot, brow furrowed, chin tucked in, as if he is about to head-butt the camera. The image is stark, shorn of the flags and fancy that have been Mr. Trump's preferred framings for photo ops at Mar-a-Lago or Trump Tower, or during his term in office, and that communicate power and the gilded glow of success." Friedman quoted historian Sean Wilentz as saying that, of the myriad of photos of Trump, it could be the most famous or notorious and serve as "the ultimate bookend to a political arc in the United States that began decades ago, with Richard Nixon's 'I am not a crook.'

–Wikipedia

• •

By Meridith McGraw, POLITICO, 02/24/2024

He insisted that Black voters had flocked to him because of the mugshot photo from his booking in the Fulton County jail. "When I did the mug shot in Atlanta, that mug shot is No. 1," Trump claimed. "You know who embraced it more than anyone else? The Black population."

Trump's appearance provided a telling illustration of how the former president sees the political motivations of Black voters. While Trump has made inroads in the community — and the crowd on Friday lapped up his remarks — there is no evidence that his criminal charges have won him their support. Similar comments made in the past have received pushback from Black voters who scoff at the comparison of his personal troubles to their experiences with the criminal justice system.

Trump says he's 'like, really smart,' 'a very stable genius'

WASHINGTON (CBSNewYork/AP) -- President Donald Trump wants people to know he's "like, really smart" and "a very stable genius," taking to Twitter Saturday morning to defend his mental fitness and boast about his intelligence after the release of a book that portrays him as a leader who doesn't understand the weight of the presidency.

In the book, former aide Steve Bannon questions Trump's competence, but the president's having none of it.

He says critics are "taking out the old Ronald Reagan playbook and screaming mental stability and intelligence."

Trump says "my two greatest assets have been mental stability and being, like, really smart."

He says going from successful businessman to reality TV star to president on his first try "would qualify as not smart, but genius .... and a very stable genius at that!"

The president's latest tweetstorm comes after the release of 'Fire And Fury: Inside The Trump White House' by Michael Wolff, detailing a turbulent and at times chaotic first year in office for Trump and his administration.

The book draws a derogatory portrait of the 45th president as an undisciplined man-child who didn't actually want to win the White House, and who spends his evenings eating cheeseburgers in bed, watching television and talking on the telephone to old friends.

Trump recently blasted his former chief strategist Steve Bannon after learning Bannon shared revealing information with Wolff.

7th Commandment
"Thou shalt not steal."

Trump Pays $2 Million to 8 Charities for Misuse of Foundation

Under a settlement, the president admitted he had used his charity to bolster his campaign and settle business debts.

By Luis Ferré-Sadurní, New York Times, Dec. 10, 2019

President Trump has paid $2 million to eight charities as part of a settlement in which the president admitted he misused funds raised by the Donald J. Trump Foundation to promote his presidential bid and pay off business debts, the New York State attorney general said on Tuesday.

The foundation's giving patterns and management came under scrutiny during Mr. Trump's run for office, and last year the New York attorney general filed a lawsuit accusing the president and his family of using the foundation as an extension of their businesses and the campaign.

The payments were part of a settlement announced last month that capped a drawn-out legal battle. In the end, the president admitted in court documents that he had used the foundation to settle legal obligations of his businesses and even to purchase a portrait of himself.

"Charities are not a means to an end, which is why these damages speak to the president's abuse of power and represent a victory for not-for-profits that follow the law," the attorney general, Letitia James, said in a statement. "Funds have finally gone where they deserve — to eight credible charities."

Last month, a state judge ordered the president to give $2 million to the eight charities, or $250,000 per charity. Under the settlement, Mr. Trump's lawyers also agreed to liquidate the Trump Foundation's remaining assets of more than $1.7 million and disburse them to those same nonprofits, which have no connection to the president or his family.

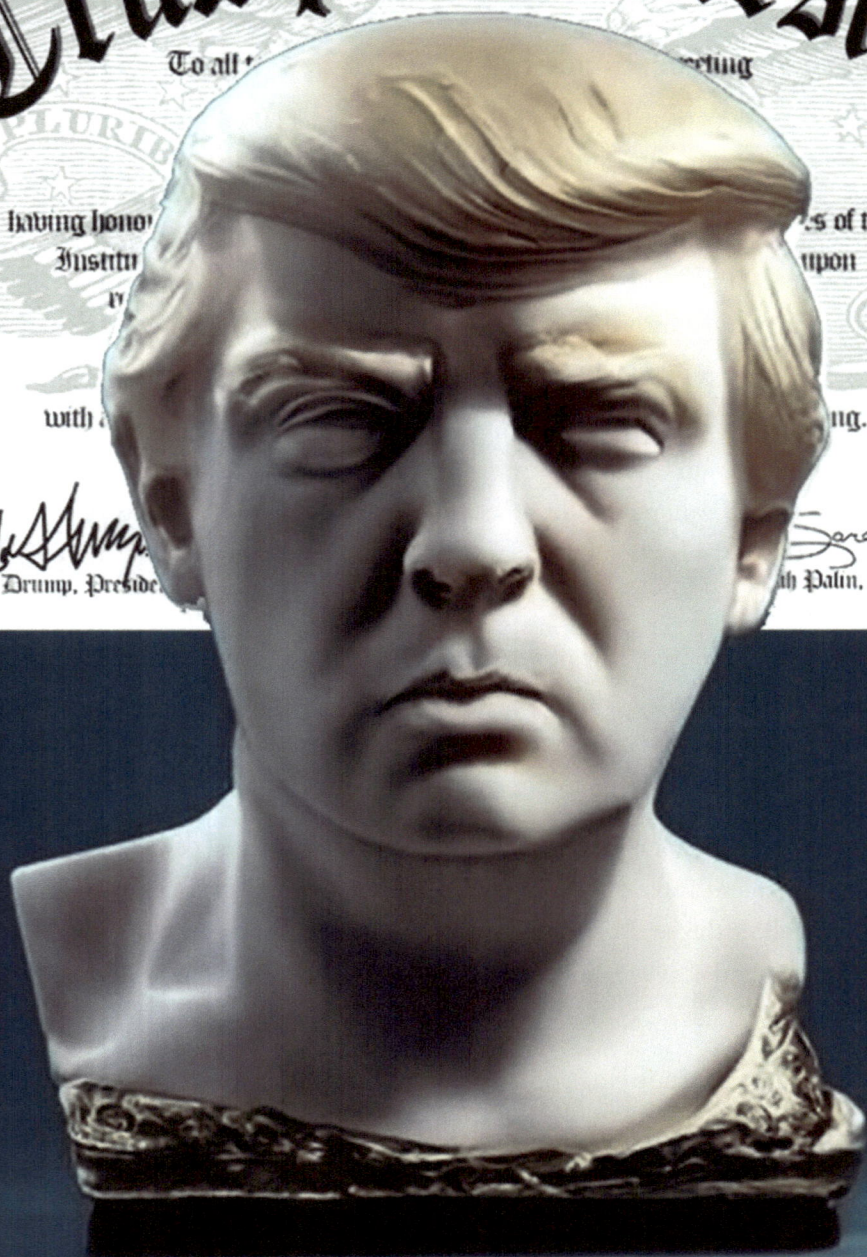

Federal court approves $25 million Trump University settlement

A federal court approved a $25 million settlement with students who said they were duped by Donald Trump and his now-defunct Trump University.

By Tom Winter and Dartunorro Clark, New York Times, Feb. 6, 2018

A federal court approved a $25 million settlement on Tuesday with students who said they were duped by Donald Trump and his now-defunct Trump University, which promised to teach them the "secrets of success" in the real estate industry.

The 9th Circuit Court of Appeals in San Francisco finalized the settlement after it was first approved by a judge last March following an appeal by Sherri Simpson, a Florida woman who said she spent roughly $19,000 on Trump University workshops. Simpson had wanted to opt out of a class action suit in order to pursue a separate suit against Trump, but the court rejected that.

Students had alleged that Trump University, which was open from 2005 to 2010, used false advertising and high-pressure sales techniques to lure them to free investor workshops at which they were sold expensive seminars and told they would be mentored by real estate gurus, leading to the loss of thousands of dollars in tuition.

A "one-year apprenticeship" at the educational institute cost $1,495; a "membership" over $10,000; and "Gold Elite" classes ran $35,000.

Trump faced two lawsuits in California and one in New York, brought by New York Attorney General Eric Schneiderman. They were folded into one class action suit after Trump was elected, according to court documents.

The cure for those who chew on pens.

The Original Dump-a-Trump Pen Holder
- Brand: Dump-a-Trump

Trump's Repeated False Attacks on Mail-In Ballots

By Eugene Kiely and Rem Rieder, FactCheck Posts, September 25, 2020

In the past 48 hours, President Donald Trump repeatedly has refused to commit to a peaceful transfer of power if he loses, claiming that mail-in voting is a "disaster" and "out of control" and suggesting without evidence that Democrats are going to steal the election.

The president repeatedly sows doubt about mail-in voting, echoing what intelligence officials have said is a Russian strategy to undermine public trust in the election.

At a Sept. 23 press briefing the president said "we're going to have to see what happens," when he was asked if he would commit to a peaceful transfer of power. "Get rid of the ballots," he said, and there would be a "very peaceful … continuation" of power.

"The ballots are out of control," he said of mail-in ballots. "You know it. And you know who knows it better than anybody else? The Democrats know it better than anybody else." He doubled down the next day, saying mail-in ballots are "a whole big scam" when asked if he would only accept the election results if he wins.

"We want to make sure the election is honest, and I'm not sure that it can be," he told reporters on Sept. 24. "I don't know that it can be with this whole situation — unsolicited ballots. They're unsolicited; millions being sent to everybody. And we'll see."

We have been tracking the president's remarks about mail-in voting. In late July, we wrote a story — "The President's Trumped-Up Claims of Voter Fraud" — recapping his numerous false, misleading and unsupported claims to date about mail-in ballots. At the time, Trump had suggested the 2020 election should be postponed, claiming mail-in voting this year will result in the "most INACCURATE & FRAUDULENT Election in history."

Oompa loompa doompety doo. You look like us with a weirder hairdo.

Trump Reportedly Does All His Own Makeup

By Kevin Fitzpatrick, Vanity Fair, February 9, 2019

Long before President Trump decried investigations of his office over Twitter, a gentler query dogged the celebrity businessman: how does he maintain his infamous orange hue, even while residing in wintry D.C.? It's a question that persists into the third year of Trump's tenure in the White House, and investigations of the matter have yielded surprising insight into the commander in chief's styling habits.

The New York Times pursued the idea as a matter of Trump's health, though a senior administration official only offered that Trump's notable tan—in February, no less—is the result of "good genes." Further investigation revealed that neither tanning beds nor spray-tan booths exist within the White House or Air Force One, at least according to senior officials. Former aide Omarosa Manigault Newman wrote in a tell-all book that Trump travels with a tanning bed, while lighter-hued circles around the president's eyes have fueled speculation that he utilizes goggles to protect himself from ultraviolet rays.

Trump's orange hue has also proven a frequent source of media ridicule, even as Saturday Night Live star Alec Baldwin has suggested makeup artists deliberately avoid exaggerating the shade—at Lorne Michaels's behest—so as "not to over-orange anything out of malice." Baldwin has otherwise described Trump's look as somewhere between "Mark Rothko orange" and a "slightly paler Orange Crush."

The president is famously self-sufficient when it comes to appearance, even detailing the elaborate process behind his signature swooping blond hair. And while an unnamed former campaign hand admitted Trump's orange glow is "a captivating story," they insisted Trump's grooming habits are his own secret to keep.

So put away all malice and all deceit and hypocrisy and envy and all slander.

1 Peter 2:1–5

Trump, Vowing 'Retribution, Foretells a Second Term of Spite

By Maggie Haberman & Shane Goldmacher, The New York Times, Mar 7, 2023

Donald J. Trump has for decades trafficked in the language of vengeance, from his days as a New York developer vowing "an eye for an eye" in the real estate business to ticking through an enemies ledger in 2022 as he sought to oust every last Republican who voted for his impeachment. "Four down and six to go," he cheered in a statement as one went down to defeat. But even though payback has long been part of his public persona, Mr. Trump's speech on Saturday at the Conservative Political Action Conference was striking for how explicitly he signaled that any return trip to the White House would amount to a term of spite.

"In 2016, I declared, 'I am your voice,'" Mr. Trump told the crowd in National Harbor, Md. "Today, I add: I am your warrior. I am your justice. And for those who have been wronged and betrayed, I am your retribution."

He repeated the phrase for emphasis: "I am your retribution."

Framing the 2024 election as a dire moment in an us-versus-them struggle — "the final battle," as he put it — Mr. Trump charged forward in an uncharted direction for American politics, talking openly about leveraging the power of the presidency for political reprisals.

His menacing declaration landed differently in the wake of the pro-Trump mob's assault on the Capitol on Jan. 6, 2021, in a last-ditch effort to keep him in power. The notion that Mr. Trump's supporters could be spurred to violence is no longer hypothetical, as it was in 2016 when he urged a rally audience to "knock the crap out of" hecklers. The attack on the Capitol underscored that his most fanatical followers took his falsehoods and claims of victimhood seriously — and were willing to act on them.alternative to overthrowing or overturning the system itself.

I've done more for Women than just about any President in history."

by Red Rosenberg, Ms. Magazine, 9/5/2020

In the tweet, Trump exclaims he has "done more for WOMEN than just about any President in HISTORY."

He didn't say he's done good things for women. He just said 'no president has done more.' And he's right. No president has done more for women— to make our lives worse!"

He's:

   "Cut funding for women's health"

   "Undermined equal pay laws"

   "Eliminated child care for military families"

   "Undermined civil rights laws"

   "Blocked Planned Parenthood funding"

   "Weirdly obsessed with being mean to Rosie O'Donnell"

   "Reversed college campus sexual assault guidelines"

   "Cheated on [all three of] his wives"

      Call particular woman:

      "UGLY"

      "FAT"

      "NASTY"

      "CRAZY"

      "DISGUSTING"

      "A LOSER"

      A "PIG"

      A DOG

      A "BIMBO"

   Called his daughter "HCT"

   "Disbanded the White House Council on Women and Girls."

"THIS MAN IS A TOTAL SEXIST"

2nd Commandment

"Thou shalt not take the name of the Lord thy God in vain"

'Using the Lord's name in vain': Evangelicals chafe at Trump's blasphemy

By Gabby Orr, POLITICO, 08/12/2019

Paul Hardesty didn't pay much attention to President Donald Trump's campaign rally in Greenville, N.C., last month until a third concerned constituent rang his cellphone. The residents of Hardesty's district — he's a Trump-supporting, West Virginia state senator — were calling to complain that Trump was "using the Lord's name in vain," Hardesty recounted.

Here's what he would have seen: Trump crowing, "They'll be hit so g--damn hard," while bragging about bombing Islamic State militants. And Trump recounting his warning to a wealthy businessman: "If you don't support me, you're going to be so g--damn poor."

To most of America, the comments went unnoticed. Instead, the nation was gripped by the moment a "send her back" chant broke out as Trump went after Somali-born Democratic Rep. Ilhan Omar, an American citizen. But some Trump supporters were more fixated on his casual use of the word "g--damn" — an off-limits term for many Christians — not to mention the numerous other profanities laced throughout the rest of his speech.might turn off the religious right.

He's been divorced twice and has faced constant allegations of extramarital affairs. He previously supported abortion rights, and he has stumbled when trying to discuss the specifics of his religious beliefs, once referring to a book in the Bible as "Two Corinthians" instead of Second Corinthians. Yet to this point, Trump has maintained broad support from evangelicals, including the unwavering backing of some prominent conservative Christian leaders.

Angertainment

By Sarah Baxter, The New Statesman, January 17, 2024

Donald Trump's favourite Hollywood role model is Sylvester Stallone. At every one of his campaign stops, there is 2024 "Make America great again" (Maga) merch on sale – flags, posters, T-shirts – showing the 77-year-old Trump as Rambo wielding his bazooka with the message "No Man, no Woman, no Commie can stump him".

Another superimposes Trump's head on to the ripped torso of Stallone's boxing champ Rocky, a meme the former president has admiringly reposted on social media.

As Rocky says, "It ain't how hard you hit… it's how hard you can get hit and keep moving forward." It's an all-American narrative that fits Trump's defiant campaign persona: a man hell-bent on revenge, channelling his grief and fury at losing the 2020 election into an all-too-plausible comeback story. And Americans can't seem to get enough of his angertainment.

The Wicked Man

In his arrogance the wicked man hunts down the weak, who are caught in the schemes he devises.

He boasts of the cravings of his heart; he blesses the greedy and reviles the LORD.

In his pride the wicked does not seek him; in all his thoughts there is no room for God.

His ways are always prosperous; he is haughty and your laws are far from him; he sneers at all his enemies.

He says to himself, "Nothing will shake me; I'll always be happy and never have trouble."

His mouth is full of curses and lies and threats; trouble and evil are under his tongue.

Psalm 10: 2-8

"I am your retribution"

By Sarah Baxter, The New Statesman, January 17, 2024

We don't know whether Trump can generate enough steam to propel him to the White House on 5 November – but it could be payback time if he wins. Trump has vowed to seek vengeance on his political enemies, on behalf of his most faithful supporters. "I am your warrior, I am your justice and for those that have been wronged and betrayed, I am your retribution," Trump proclaimed last March.

It was tempting to laugh. The idea that a self-obsessed billionaire who shamelessly peddles lies about having won the last election could embody the assorted grievances of millions of Americans seemed preposterous. But who doesn't dream of revenge and redemption? Voters are angry about the lost years under Covid, the 2.4 million immigrants apprehended at the southern border last year, and the high inflation – now curbed at 3.4 per cent – that has led to punitive borrowing costs and mortgage rates of around 7 per cent. For his fans, a Trump restoration would present a stirring climax to the greatest political show on Earth.

At the end of 2023, the Daily Mail asked 1,000 likely US voters to sum up in one word what Biden and Trump would want in a second term as president. For Biden, the most common response was "nothing", followed by "economy", "peace" and "democracy". For Trump, it was "revenge" (the next-most frequent words were "power", "economy" and "dictatorship").

But it is striking how few senior members of his former administration believe he can be trusted with power again. According to John Kelly, his former White House chief of staff, Trump often wanted the Department of Justice to prosecute those who crossed him, but his requests were ignored. "The lesson the former president learned from his first term is don't put guys like me... in those jobs," Kelly told the Washington Post in November. " The lesson he learned was to find sycophants."

If he loses the election in November, Donald Trump has plenty of hardcore supporters already flirting with the prospect of civil war. If he wins, he may never give up power voluntarily. It sounds absurd, but Trump has suggested the "stolen" election of 2020 entitles him to a constitution-defying third term in office. For him, revenge is a never-ending story.

www.ingramcontent.com/pod-product-compliance
Lightning Source LLC
Chambersburg PA
CBHW042301040326
40677CB00034B/756